KATHARINE PAYNE

ELEPHANTS CALLING

CROWN PUBLISHERS, INC. • *New York*

For Damon, Sarah, and Jacob, who live in
America, where there have been no wild
elephants for the last 10,000 years

For the children of Sengwa, the children
of Amboseli, and other African children who
know wild elephants in their own countries.

In Africa, in Kenya,
there is a mountain called Kilimanjaro.
At the foot of Kilimanjaro lies
a land of many elephants.
People call the land Amboseli,
which means "salty dust."
They named it for a place
where an ancient lake
dried up thousands of years ago,
leaving a barren, salty, dusty pan.
But not far from the pan there are
swamps where elephants drink
all year long.
The elephants,
if they were naming the land,
might call it "always water."

3

There are also grassy plains in Amboseli, and groves of thorny acacia trees, where elephants eat and sleep. It was in one of those groves, on a sweet breezy morning in January—African summer—that Raoul was born.

His head and back were covered with soft reddish hair. His trunk was short and floppy. His legs were wobbly.

Before he was one day old, Raoul could stand up in his house and that's where he is standing now. The roof is the underside of his mother's belly, and her four strong legs are the corners. Only a very young baby fits in that house. His four-year-old sister has to stand outside.

Their mother's breasts are full of milk for them both.

No other elephant looks just like Raoul's mother. She has a full tail, upcurving tusks, a notch in her left ear, a lump at the top of her front left leg (where Raoul's trunk is pointing), and a sharp angle between her brow and the top of her head. Her name is Renata.

Raoul knows Renata from the way she looks and smells, from the sound of her voice and the taste of her milk, and from how she feels when he touches her. Babies and mothers have delicate ways of communicating with each other.

When Raoul leans his trunk against Renata's front leg, she lets him nurse.

Raoul's sister, brother, grandmother, two great-aunts, two aunts, and six cousins are all close by. There are no older male elephants, called bulls, to be seen. Elephant fathers do not live with their families, and brothers go off on their own when they get to be about fourteen years old. But female elephants never leave the family into which they are born. They spend their whole life as a group, taking care of each other and their babies.

Raoul's grandmother has had a mud bath. The dried mud that covers her face keeps the insects off and protects her skin from sunburn. She is more than fifty years old. She knows hundreds of other elephants. She knows hundreds of paths between the acacia forests and the cool swamps, and hundreds of smells of friends, family, and enemies. She knows the signs of plenty and the signs that grasses and elephants are growing thin and thirsty. She knows the energy and sudden tiredness of young elephants and the sound of hunger in a lion's voice. She remembers secret places where elephants can dig for water when other places have gone dry.

Raoul's relatives stay near the grandmother. They all listen when she listens and stop when she stops. When she moves, they usually follow. As the oldest elephant in the family, she often makes decisions for everybody. She is called the matriarch.

Raoul's older sister is watching him. Someone always watches him, often from no farther away than the length of his own tail.

If Raoul starts to wander away, if he falls down, squeals or growls, his sister will make a gruff sound in her throat. The older relatives will answer with a chorus of rumbling calls, and some of them will come running to see what's wrong.

There's a lot of company for an elephant calf, but no privacy.

People have been studying elephants in Amboseli for many years, and this is why Raoul has a human name. Everyone in Raoul's family was given a name starting with *R*. Elephants in other families got names beginning with other letters.

The elephant study was done in a simple way. A small truck stayed near the elephants day after day. Inside the truck, a person wrote down the names of the elephants she saw and what they were doing. She never got out of the truck, even when she wanted to stretch, or cool off, or get a better look. She stayed in the truck so as not to frighten, not to attract, and not even to interest the elephants.

The person who started the study was Cynthia Moss. Later she was joined by another researcher, Joyce Poole.

Over several years, the elephants got used to having a truck around. They scratched against it as if it were a rock. They seemed not to notice there was a living person inside watching them.

◁ Tom, an elephant bull, visits the Amboseli research camp and looks at Joyce Poole, who looks at him.

▽ Left: Joyce at work. Right: Targa, a one-year-old Asian elephant calf, meets me and my research partner Bill Langbauer in a circus. Targa helped us learn that elephants make infrasound.

It is amazing how much you can learn about animals if you watch for a long time without disturbing them. They do odd things, which at first you don't understand. Then gradually your mind opens to what it would be like to have different eyes, different ears, and different taste; different needs, different fears, and different knowledge from ours.

Elephants, for instance, use a special kind of sound called infrasound. It is very, very low sound, so low that people cannot hear it. But sometimes people can *feel* it, because it makes the air throb. You may have noticed this feeling when there is close, rumbly thunder.

Nobody knew that elephants use infrasound until just a few years ago, when I happened to notice something in a zoo. I noticed a throbbing in the air near the elephants' cages. It reminded me of something from my childhood, when I used to sing in a church choir. My place was in front of the organ pipes that made the very deepest, lowest notes. When the organist played these notes, the air around me would throb and flutter. The lower down the notes went, the less I could hear them, and yet I could still feel the air throbbing. I was reaching the bottom of what human ears can hear.

In the zoo I felt the same thing again, without any sound. I guessed the elephants might be making powerful sounds like an organ's notes, but even lower in pitch.

To test this guess, two friends and I made tape recordings of the elephants in the zoo and also of elephants in a circus, using equipment that could record infrasound. The recordings showed that my guess was right. And with that, my life with elephants had begun.

11

Joyce Poole invited me to Amboseli to record the calls of the elephants whom she and Cynthia knew so well.

Now there were two of us in the truck. We kept track of which elephants were near us all the time, what they were doing, and what we heard, while I made tape recordings, as I had done in the zoo.

Sometimes we heard low calls that sounded like purring or rumbling. Sometimes we partly heard and partly felt an elephant call. Sometimes when we heard a call, we knew which elephant was calling. But our ears are only human, not like elephant ears, which hear low-pitched sounds very well. Our tapes recorded three times more elephant calls than we were able to hear.

Some of the calls we couldn't hear were made by the elephants we were watching, but others were made by elephants that were far away. For infrasound is special in another way, too: it travels farther than the sounds that we hear. It travels so well that elephants can hear each other's low calls even when they are miles apart.

What is it like to have a voice that travels over the horizon? What is it like to hear other elephants calling from miles away? I was wondering about things like this as Joyce and I bumped along in her truck on February 4, 1985, the morning when we first saw Raoul.

▽ Left: *I join Joyce in the truck.* Right: *testing our tape recorder, microphones, and battery before putting them into the trunk.*

Raoul might have liked to spend the whole day in the cool acacia shade drinking Renata's sweet, plentiful milk. But elephant calves must go where their mothers go. Renata and all the other older elephants are thirsty and about to set out for the swamp.

"*Purrrrrrrrr.*"

"*Purr.*"

"*Purrrrr.*"

The air fills with soft rumbles. We hear them from the left, and right, and all around the truck. The big elephants who were scattered among the trees now stop pulling down leaves and branches. Every mother's calf moves to her side. All the mothers start to move, not at the same time but in the same direction. That way, miles ahead, lies the swamp.

Traveling with babies is a slow business. It is not long before Raoul asks for a rest. He touches Renata's front leg. Renata stops, and then everybody stops. The young calves lie down in the shade under the bellies of their mothers.

Soon the older elephants get sleepy too. Without lying down, they drowse. One old aunt coils her trunk up and rests the coil on her tusks. Another lets her trunk droop to the ground. The longer she sleeps, the longer her trunk gets.

With eyes still closed, the older elephants throw dust over their backs. It gets dusty down in the bedroom, but the babies sleep on and on.

Eventually it is the calves who decide that naptime is over. First Raoul's cousin pounces on him...

Then his sister boosts him to his feet with her trunk. *"Oooffffffff!"*

Raoul's family is not the only family making its way toward water this morning.

All across Amboseli, other thirsty elephants are doing the same thing. Big families, middle-sized families, and small families are all slowly moving toward the Amboseli swamps and water holes, eating, resting, and nursing as they go.

As the elephants move, their trunks swing back and forth, searching the ground for smells. Dung, old urine, and tracks are full of news. The elephants gather news of friends, of relatives, of strangers; of lions and warthogs and many other animals. For even though the animals who passed earlier are no longer there, they have left messages that the elephants are reading, in a smell language that they understand.

The air too is full of smells, and suddenly Raoul's relatives all sniff high over their heads. They stop in their tracks and perk their ears.

We see nothing, but the air begins to throb with calls that Joyce and I cannot hear. Then Renata bellows. Everyone else rumbles and trumpets and runs forward. The F family—Fernanda, Felicity, and their relatives—are ahead!

Whenever the R and F families meet, there is a party!

At the swamp everyone in both families is happy. Here a young elephant has everything: family, milk, mud, things to chase, new friends…

including Fiona, just Raoul's size. Raoul might like to stay all day.

But as soon as Raoul's relatives have quenched their thirst, they get hungry. There is not enough to eat near the swamp. What can the family do, except set out on another walk?

"Purrrr-R-R-R-R-r-r-r-r." It is the matriarch's voice. Partway along a smooth bare trail that leads away from the swamp, Raoul's grandmother calls without looking back at her family. To my ears, which cannot hear infrasound, her calls sound soft and fluttery. But to elephants they are deep, steady rumbles, meaning "Let's go."

"Purrrrrrrrr-r-r-r-r-r-r-r-r-r-r-r-r."

Renata and the great-aunts, the aunts, their daughters and nieces, slowly finish drinking, nudge their children with trunks and feet, murmur, and start up the trail.

Raoul does not want to leave. He sucks his trunk.

"PurrRRRr-r-r-r-r, purrrr-r-r, purrrrrrr." Now all the elephants in the family call at once. The matriarch claps and scrapes her ears against her neck, and everyone starts to walk, their backs swaying and their feet scuffling in the sandy soil.

The matriarch's "let's go" calls are signals only for the R family. Fiona and her relatives stay at the swamp.

Raoul takes one backward look over his shoulder at Fiona and follows his mother.

Sitting in the truck, I feel sorry that the families must separate so soon. But perhaps it is not quite so hard for the elephants. For elephants can be joined by their deep voices even when they are separated by a forest.

◁ *Branches from acacia trees are a favorite food of the Amboseli elephants. Here a tough old female with one tusk is breaking a branch by stepping on one end and pulling the other end with her trunk. Then she stuffs it into her mouth, thorns and all.*

After elephant families separate for feeding, they stay far enough apart that they rarely compete for food. This is especially important during the five rainless months of every year, when grasses and leaves are dry and scarce. With hundreds of elephants moving from area to area, staying apart cannot be easy. If families did not know where other families were, it might often happen that too many would gather in one place. Then there would not be enough food to go around.

Certain families seem to plan their patterns of movement with each other. While keeping a mile or two of forest or grassland between them, they move parallel to each other for days and days, changing directions at the same time as they feed. They stay far enough away so that they don't compete for food, yet close enough to hear and respond if anyone calls for help.

Would such things be possible if elephants were not listening all the time with their huge sensitive ears to each other's far-traveling voices?

What is this?

Spread out along the trail, Raoul and his relatives have silently stopped and are holding as still as if they were frozen. Their heads are high, and their ears are tall and wide.

Now they move again—now they freeze again.

They are listening. All together, they hold so still that the faintest sounds, sounds even from miles away, will reach their ears. A few more steps and they freeze again.

This much listening is unusual. Who is on the trail ahead?

Elephant bulls.

Bulls doing the work of bulls. They are sorting out who is stronger than whom.

Not long from now Raoul, too, will start doing the same thing that all bulls do. He will start challenging every little bull he meets to a pushing contest and remembering who won last time.

Twenty years from now he will be taller than any female. His head will be broader and rounder, and his tusks will be thicker. He will have moved to a place where only males live and for the rest of his life he will see his family only for brief visits.

▷ *Young elephant bulls test each other's strength in pushing contests.*

Most of his meetings with other bulls will be fairly calm. But during part of each year Raoul will be in a strange condition called "musth." Then, like great Pablo here, he will be stronger than the bulls that are not in musth and will fight in earnest with other musth bulls. The glands in front of Raoul's ears will leak out a liquid that says in smell language, *"I am Raoul in musth. Look out!"* His back feet will be wet with another liquid that says the same thing.

Independent at last, Raoul will leave all other elephants and travel alone. Holding his chin in and his head high, swaggering and taking enormous steps, he will walk back and forth across Amboseli, searching for fights or females. He will make strange gravelly voiced calls that males make only when they are in musth. Across the plain other musth males will be listening. Some of them will change direction to get out of his way; others will answer.

△ *This bull, with the musth liquid on his cheek, walks just behind his mate.*

Raoul will freeze in his tracks to listen. Certain kinds of answers to his musth rumbles will cause him to turn, find the other bull, and fight. His ears will be folded in a terrible "V," which announces that he is in a rage. He and his adversary will charge at each other, clashing tusks again and again, until one of them runs away with his head low and his tail out straight.

And if Raoul becomes the biggest undefeated musth bull in Amboseli, the prize that every bull wants will be his. The prize is a chance to mate. The stronger Raoul grows, the more mates he will have. He will be able to find mates by listening for the far-traveling calls that female elephants make only when they are ready to mate.

Raoul will guard his mate, as the big bull in the picture above, with the musth liquid on his cheek, is doing; and she will walk just ahead of Raoul, looking backward out of the corner of her eye to signify that she has also chosen him. None of the other bulls will dare come close.

Raoul will walk long distances but eat very little during the months when he is in musth. Then hunger will come. His musth liquids will stop flowing. For the rest of the year he will feel more peaceful, while other bulls come into musth and have their chance to mate.

What do you think about all this, Raoul?

Raoul isn't paying attention. In the midst of all the ruckus he has given his brother and sister, his grandmother, mother, great-aunts, aunts, and cousins the slip. For three minutes he has been out in the world by himself.

Not far away, Raoul's relatives are watching the fighting elephant bulls. In the truck, Joyce and I are watching them too. We have all forgotten Raoul.

But he does not stay out of our thoughts for long. For suddenly, from the direction in which he disappeared, there comes a blood-curdling scream. At that very moment, a terrified warthog bolts through the elephant herd heading for the plain and disappears in a cloud of dust.

Renata, hearing her son's scream, gives a mighty roar. Elephants in all directions answer Renata, and then they answer each other with roars, screams, bellows, trumpets, and rumbles.

In the truck, Joyce and I are surrounded by running, screaming elephants. Male and female elephants of all sizes and ages charge past each other and us with eyes wide, foreheads high, trunks, tails, and ears swinging wildly. The truck is smothered in dust. The air throbs with infrasound made not only by elephants' voices but also by their thundering feet. Running legs and swaying bodies loom toward and above us and veer away at the last second. Will we be trampled flat?

And where is Raoul?

It is much later in the day before we find out.

Raoul's relatives are closely packed together, showing that they have been very frightened. Liquid is running down their cheeks from the glands in front of their ears—the same glands that make musth liquid for males—which also shows that they have been very frightened. But their little calves are still with them.

Renata does not seem angry at Raoul. Perhaps elephants don't ask for explanations.

But *I* would like to know what happened. It was clear from the position of Raoul's trunk as he started exploring that he was following his sense of smell. Did the rich, unfamiliar smell of a warthog in its burrow lead him to put his trunk in, hoping to learn more? Did the warthog inside, seeing a long, wiggly thing in its doorway, panic and bolt out? Was this what caused Raoul's wild screams of surprise and terror?

We don't know the answers. We just feel tired, like all the elephants. Days that don't go according to the matriarch's plan are tiring. It is a relief that by late afternoon things are getting back to normal.

Night is coming on. Raoul's family is settling down in an acacia grove about a mile from where they began the day.

The calves have nursed; they are full of milk. Raoul is in his house. Everyone is ready for a night's rest.

The evening is quiet. The air is still. Renata's voice—the same voice that reached elephants far over the hills a few hours ago—is making a soft little humming sound. It is a sound that an elephant mother only makes when she has a very young calf. It is a soft, soft sound, just loud enough to be heard by someone no farther away than the length of an elephant's tail.

But Raoul doesn't hear any elephants calling at all. He is asleep.

INDEX

"I was born in America, in Ithaca, New York, a mile from where I now live. My parents, brother, sister, and I had a farm. There were fields and gardens, chickens, sheep, pigs, cows, dogs, cats, a pony, and a lot of work to do. A stream with waterfalls ran through our land, and I spent my best days exploring.

"I went to Cornell University, where I studied music and biology, and met a musical biologist who became my husband. Together we studied the behavior of humpback whales—whales that sing beautiful songs in the ocean every spring. When we studied whales on the wild coast of Argentina, our four children came with us. Some of our expeditions lasted for years. The children missed ordinary school, but they saw things and lived in places that none of us will ever forget.

"One day, in a zoo, I made a discovery about elephants, which is described in this book. Since then I have been working far from the sea in three African countries—Kenya, Namibia, and Zimbabwe—trying to learn about elephants and their communication.

"People use oil that they get from whales and ivory that they get from elephants. These things are worth a great deal of money. But they cost more than money—they cost life itself. I think that is too great a price to pay for oil and ivory, so I try to help people understand what the world is losing. It is losing deep voices—and some of the richest sounds that have ever been heard are in the songs of whales. It is losing great listeners—and the most intense listening I have ever observed is the listening of elephants, which unites and bonds their peaceful society.

"I dream that a day will come when people will value wild animals not for money but for who they are and what we can learn from them. If we learn to listen as often and as well as elephants do, it is possible that listening will keep the world safe. Safe for us in our cities and villages and farms; and the great-voiced animals in the oceans and forests and plains."

—Katy Boynton Payne

Text copyright © 1992 by Katharine Payne
Photograph on page 11 by Nancy Adams. Photograph on page 12 (right) by Jen and Des Bartlett. Photograph on page 16 (bottom) © Tim Fitzharris/AllStock. Photographs on pages 19 (right), 28 & 29 © by W. R. Langbauer, Jr. Photograph on page 30 by Bianca Lavies, © National Geographic Society. Photograph on page 18 by Lysa Leland. Photograph on page 12 (left) by Joyce Poole. Photograph on pages 21 (bottom) by Philip Stander. All other photographs copyright © 1992 by Katharine Payne.

Published by Crown Publishers, Inc., a Random House company, 225 Park Avenue South, New York, New York 10003
CROWN is a trademark of Crown Publishers, Inc.   Manufactured in Hong Kong
Library of Congress Cataloging-in-Publication Data
Payne, Katharine.
    Elephants calling / Katharine Payne.
        p.   cm.
    Summary: The author describes her discovery that elephants communicate with low-frequency calls that are inaudible to humans.
    1. Elephants—Behavior—Juvenile literature. 2. Animal communication—Juvenile literature. [1. Elephants. 2. Animal communication.]
I. Title.
QL737.P98P39   1992
599.6′10459—dc20   91-34547
ISBN 0-517-58175-2 (trade)
    0-517-58176-0 (lib. bdg.)   10 9 8 7 6 5 4 3 2 1   First Edition